The Final Step

The Final Step

Musings of Mind and Spirit

J. MICHAELS

RESOURCE *Publications* · Eugene, Oregon

THE FINAL STEP
Musings of Mind and Spirit

Resource Publications
An Imprint of Wipf and Stock Publishers
199 W. 8th Ave., Suite 3
Eugene, OR 97401

www.wipfandstock.com

ISBN 13: 978-1-61097-116-4

Manufactured in the U.S.A.

To those fair souls who have pursued these words;
May they bring you peace and lead you to still waters.

Contents

Preface

Tᴴɪꜱ ɪꜱ ᴍʏ ᴄᴏɴᴄʟᴜᴅɪɴɢ step. Two years ago, I took the first step. I awoke at dream's insistence and wrote the first of a thousand poems and odes, all received in similar fashion and written by my untrained hand. Nine blank journals filled with stories of love, mind, paradise, and absurdity. The "love and paradise" part is certainly straightforward and causes little censure among the open-hearted. Yet some take issue with the grappling of the mind and the revealing and uprooting of the absurdities that constitute many of our most basic assumptions.

Despite a world that continually uses those absurdities to deny truth, Heaven, and the reality of a non-physical mind, I defy anyone to reject love. You might as well sever your hands as you serve yourself as to deny the essence of true life. Life is certainly not worth the living if not for the unifying presence of love. Yet some may still fear it. They may shy away from its depth. Yet we all seek it as savior, albeit as popular country fare states, in all the wrong places.

Within the rubble of the world's odious walls that I seek to tear down, I hope you will find freedom. In these words I offer, I pray you may take heart. For if the material life has offended thee, let it be known it is false and cannot obviate love. One, and only one, reality truly exists. We have chosen to ignore its glimpse. Instead, we have opted for the world's offer of its insanity soup; constituted of death, poverty, violence, and discord.

So I write this one last book of tales, hoping you will agree, praying for truth recognition and all that it will bring. Bear with me, this one last time, as I bow to your pleasure and present some final rhyme. It may or may not tickle your fancy. It may or may not remind you of your sacred Home. But if you dare to read on, you may find your soul rearranged. Taken apart and reassembled in grace, you may just find yourself headed in a different direction.

May our Father bless us all and may we never leave His Sight. May we arrive Home at last, finally getting it right. Namaste and Godspeed, my sister/brother. Someday, we all end up on the ultimate threshold and take that final step to redemption. Let us set our bearings together and travel its passage in less lonely terms.

Who Do You Love

Who do you love of all your children
The one in front of you, of course
The one that is apparent to you
And assures a lack of remorse
For there is but One anyway
So peer no further, my brother
See what our Father sees
See one in the same, each in the other

Different Directions

I write to those who attune to it
The others won't get this far
The ones who do will flourish
The others pursue a divergent star

I'm not all that worried
We'll arrive all in the same place
Becoming our Self in the process
Adopting all the same pace

The paths may vary and sway
Footsteps pointed in different directions
Yet converging along the way
Occupying the same space some day

Sightless Effect

A ghostly intermediary
With sightless effect
Turning pleasure into pain
If that is what we elect

Buried beneath layers of belief
Abiding in the dark places
Lies guilt attached to cause and effect
Stitching wounds with shrinking laces

The connection missed by conscious mind
No link or effect in sight
The guilt turns us from the light
Denying us a decent plight

So doubt not you have it
It is but certain fact
Forgive yourself its illusion
Let us take a different tact

We recognize that God does love us
And He is perfect, we know
So for Him to truly know us
He sees no guilty soul

We must, as well, become sightless
And see no less than love
Let guilt no longer betray us
Make clear our way above

A Dance No Doubt

No doubt, it's a dance
A wonderful, fleeting dance
I have seen but a particle of
This sweet, divine romance

I see a glint of God
His Spirit, His Love, His Soul
Starting to sense a change
About to make me whole

I may go or stay
I know not at this lovely day
But we shall never part
Of one Mind and Spirit we stay

Gnat on My Ass

It's a gnat on my ass
A bite, a nibble, then gone
If not of God this ego bears
Then I am having none

Be gone, you little nothing
A ripple on illusion's wave
I'll have no part of this hoax
I have greater things to say

Exquisite Versatility

You have exquisite versatility
My oldest and dearest Friend
I'm amazed at your invincibility
And where the endless begins
I have grown to come to know You
We are one in the same, I find
If we get too much closer
I think my life here will end
I'll take my chances, dear Heart
To be of You *is* my loving end

Glimpses of the Unlimited

I've had glimpses of the Unlimited
I will never be the same
I dismiss all past blindness
It's nice to be finally sane

We J

Hey J, did you write this book
No way j, never took a look

So was it you j, did you write it
Hey J, there's simply no way

If it wasn't J
And it wasn't j
It must have been We J

A Realm of Endless Stock

Enter the realm of knowledge
The Mind without a frame
A point of reference so vast
Eternity and it are the same

No analysis, no calculations, no fee
Nothing to figure out
No place to look for answers
To questions of *what about...*

You simply know
That is all
There when you need it
Preventing all falls

It sure is a lot easier
When certainty exists
To know what is needed
To need not insist
On nuclear responses
On keys to doors unlocked
There is nothing to acquire
In a realm of endless stock

Leaving the World of Men

I care not for where I've been
But only for who I am
To name the stairs is meaningless
They but lead to where I stand

I have arrived at the beginning
The one I long thought lost
Completing my rounded journey
I have returned at prolonged cost

Now I stand with knocker poised
To rap upon my Father's door
The prodigal son has returned
Wise enough to leave no more

As I stand there in anticipation
The door opens on its own
Standing there before me
All whom I love and Home

It's good to be Home, my brother
At long last, journey's end
Leaving the world behind me
Leaving the world of men
Able to finally say, *amen*

A Fine Attitude

I'm here to reinforce *The Course*
I know the guy that wrote it
He gave me some lucid pointers
To keep my writing fit

They are love born of love
Both do hold the key
To show this way to Heaven
To show us how to be

So procure them both, you lucky dude
They'll clean up your mind
And deliver a fine attitude

Pale and Shackled Feet

He's pulling loose the tethers
Unhooking my pale and shackled feet
Removing the cuffs of materialism
Teaching the most divine of feats
Showing me the way out of town
Pointing towards the portal of truth
Washing me over with love
Guiding to welcome Paradise
Ascending to Father above

Bird Song

The warbler serenades me
Enchanted by her silvery voice
Blinded by golden breastplate
I listen, there is no choice

More wondrous sounds
Not ever to me delivered
Tones to grace my ear
Flowing as music's river

Carrying beauty on its wings
And giving her truth away
We are brothers, tiny flyer
Joined in a natural way

Heaven's Mysts

If you have faith
You enable it
If you do not
You disable it
So decide what you want
Take it inside your heart
Then put your mind to it
Let faith do its part
For it will open doors
Not even known to exist
Revealing locales magnificent
Crowned by Heaven's Mysts

Genderless Parents

We are genderless parents
The Christ and I
Begetting thoughts quite wonderful
The sex of it gets me high
For this is truth, my brother
We are Thoughts in the Eye of God
Blessed and holy we are formed
Graced by our Father's Touch
Made of the finest finery
Who knew we were so much

Have We Forgotten

Have we forgotten
The Source from whence we came
Have we forgotten
The peace we once but claimed
Have we forgotten
The joy that was our right
Have we forgotten
The day without a night
Have we forgotten
Exactly who we are
The holy divine being
Underneath the roles and play
Have we forgotten
There is but one place to stay
Let us remember
The Christ we are this day

Something My Soul Doth Feel

I know my Father is knowable
The only question is when
I will let my faith so guide me
Until such time as then
My heart swells in anticipation
My mind glows in sweet appeal
I know my Father is knowable
It is something my soul doth feel

Poem Pop

Don't know, no, when a poem's gonna pop
Don't know, no, which way to hop
Don't know, no, if it'll ever stop
Don't know, no, when a poem's gonna pop

Secret Thoughts

I'll belch and I'll fart
Might well blow myself apart
Yet I'm not well prepared for the fallout
Of something with that much tart

So restrain myself I will
I'll tender no more your pride
These secret thoughts are best well hidden
Keep them all inside

Yet pay caution, my brother
Inside does not blow you apart
Causing tremors that trouble your heart

Tickle Tickle

Perhaps we'll give our dear brothers
A giggle, a chuckle or two
Keep mentioning those unmentionables
See if it tickles them true
If it rubs the funny bone
If a smile it doth make
It will be worth the time imparted
And the joke it surely faked
It assures you, my brother
Of yourself, don't seriously take
The Christ in you is the only
Voice which you need partake

Enough for All

The currency of the world
Should bother neither you or I
We have so much in store for us
So much to fill the eye
Wondrous things within
Such as that you've never seen
Enough to obviate the false
And fill our lowly means
We have enough to pay
For that which incurs no fee
We have enough to give away
Enough for all to see

Poetic License

Poetic license, poetic license
Freedom for you and me
To explore mind so open
With words that come so free

They are divinely sent, my brother
They are pearls among the less
Meant to calm our minds
Make our hearts ache less

Let us partake of their goodness
Assume they are part of We
Let them enter your heart
And teach us how to be

A Derivative of Two

Joy is mine, sweet Brother
My heart does sing most well
To be in love with You
Closes forever, the door to hell

Happiness is not an illusion
It is obtainable for me and you
Join my sweet Brother and I
Share the joy that is our due
Know the bliss of oneness
As The One derives from the two

Rhyming Keys

I strain to rhyme at times, my friends
Unable to let it arrive here
Unable to let it in

Tis an omen to me, it is
That I have become the less
I've tinkered with other beings
And disconnected from how I'm blessed

Yet when I open my heart
The words do start to flow
The rhyme and rhythm are quite natural
It takes us where we need to go
To accept that lovingly given
Is a gift beyond what we know
A key to the door to Heaven
A key to what we need to know

A Lot More Fun

No matter what you do
No matter your course of life
I will forever love you

A mere compensation I ask
To forgive whatever you see
Forgive as if it never happened
Refuse to let it be

For it is simple distraction
A lie for our eyes and mind
For all that ever happened
Hid truth and left it behind

We have but to claim our brotherhood
And see ourselves as one
Close our eyes to the lowly false
For truth that is a lot more fun

No Better Gift

Completely in Thy Will
Is where I will to be
Completely in Thy Will
Is the only place for me
I am Yours Father
I leave any will of my own
I am Yours Father
I want nothing left to own
I am Your Son, my Beloved
The best that I would be
I am Your Son, dear Father
No better gift could I receive

Look For Joy to Stay

When the world no longer satisfies
When its offerings begin to pale
When pain overcomes the pleasure
When it starts to look like hell

It may be time to turn away
And look for a better way
It may be time to seek the truth
And look for a brighter day

The answer, my friend, is simple
As turning to God and pray
Asking for *His* Will to be done
And waiting for happiness to obey

You will find upon investigation
The world does surely lack
We will find our only happiness
When to it, we turn our backs
And look towards sweet Heaven
And ask of our Father, *His* Way
Listen for the holy answer
And look for joy to stay

The Most Amazing Hands

This love that reaches out to me
Has the most amazing hands
They carry such gifts as those
I can barely understand
Yet they fill me up
They carry me to greater heights
In the direction of my Home
Towards those celestial lights
They will deliver me safely
Into the Heart of God
They will gently lay me down
Caress my face, touch my soul
Deliver me unto eternity
Reaching my final goal

The Proper Other

You might not like it
When I belch and fart and such
But heed the intent, my brother
And know there is wisdom much
For I use these *dirty little words*
To stir up the stew of your mind
I use then fast and loosely
They may come in varied rhyme
Yet they are surely pearls
Pearls of a different color
See them just as clearly
As you do the proper other

Superficial Differences

All differences are superficial
They deny the truth of We
Born to separate and divide
They are wholly untrue we see

If you could but see the oneness
That lies beyond the lies
You would agree, the differences
Can bear no truth on high

Made solely to confuse
To deny our Heavenly due
Made to keep us apart
And prevent the loving of you

Forgiven Now

It is forgiven now
The one mistake I made
The one bad choice taken
The one most grossly paid

It's been a long time coming
A long time to hate one's self
Forgiven now, the price so great
Assuming now, Christ's true Self

Perfect Solutions

It's hard to recognize perfect solutions
But I'm starting to
Tis difficult to perceive the truth
But I want to
An uphill battle all the way
I know is not true
For I am now on level ground
Watching them all come through

Something to Think About

I hope our odes do give you
Something to think about
I pray they have dearly touched you
And caused redemption to come about
I would like to know the outcome
Of words that ring your heart
I would like to know the answer
Of why you stand apart
I would like to know your thinking
About this lonely farce

What Being Our Own god Entails

We've learned what separation brings
We've found what being our own god entails
We're aware of what this life has been
We know how much it fails

I recommend we take a different route
A path that few have known
I say let's chance it anyway
Perchance to lead us Home

Sure as Shirley

Sure as Shirley
I'll be around sometime
We'll meet up as we planned
Back in the ancient times

We have known each other long
And we have known each other well
We've known each other so much
It makes it hard to tell
Whether we are one or two
Whether our souls do meld

So see us as one, my brother
Ignore all that is more
For to see only sweet oneness
Is to live in Paradise once more

Illusion of Being

Remembering what never was
Anticipating what never will be
Trapped in an illusion of being
Someplace that never can be

For truth, my brothers
Resides in that place between
It lives only in the present
The place where love is seen

All the rest is distraction
And doesn't truly exist
It but harbors guilt, it does
And the clenched and raged fist

So put aside all that never was
Worry not about what will be
Live simply and in the present
And God is what you'll see

A Single Word

It's just a word
No matter what I say
A collection of letters
Brought back from disarray
Combined with their collective mates
Forming up into a word
To use for good or evil
Assuming they do get heard
We end up with lines continued
Into phrases and such
Turning them as we like to
It might not mean that much
Yet if we use them rightly
Disowned of harm in our hearts
We may assemble in poem or prose
That which may combine the parts
Of the race we now call human
Bringing together disparate souls
Forming into a single word
One that reflects the Whole

Keeping Happiness Hid

Mr. Do, Do, Do
That was the previous me
Mr. Go, Go, Go
That was my basic identity
What I was doing
And where I was going
I know not in the least
It felt like an endless treadmill
Always chasing the beast
The beast may have been dollar
It may have dressed as love
It may have been based on lust
Perhaps the position above
A bigger house, a faster car
Lots of pretty dresses
Lots of food at fancy places
None of those ugly messes
I hope you find it
For I never did
It seems to get empty real fast
It seems to keep happiness hid

The United Way

We are Americans
And global citizens too
We belong to various chapters
Looking for a similar view

The secret handshake we agreed on
Our circle of friends as well
Those we approve of and lie for
Those who refuse to tell
The rules we all swore to obey
That ones that align us in groups
But decline to let us stay

And with all that grouping and ungrouping
We retreat further each day
And we will until we know better
And regroup the united way

My Human Puny Self

I am much greater
Than my human puny self
Far much grander
That any impish elf
A bag of bones and flesh
Is all it totals to
Some hair and teeth thrown in
And you have the outer you
As you may guess
It really doesn't do a thing
For all that claims and drives it
The puny self doth bring

Authentic You

Live a life you won't regret
Live it straight and true
Ask God to direct it
And become the authentic you

I Need Do Nothing

Welcome Father
Come to me as I to You
I need do nothing
For this to be true
You are Me
And I am You
I need do nothing
For this to be true

Do It Well

I do it with Christ
I have no other form
The body is a lie to me
Though it is the obvious norm

I do it only with Christ
I have no other desire
I will mate with no other
Only He lights my fire

I do it but with Christ
But if you please as well
I will do it with you, my friend
But first you must turn from hell
Meet me in love, in Christ
From there, we will all do it well

You know we're talking metaphorically.
You know that, right?
If word gets around too fast,
The hot tub will get a bit tight.

When We Close These Pages

You nasty, nasty boy, you
You've done it once again
Managing to enliven the absurd
With some sense of failing sin
I do love your sense of humor
I cherish it more than I know
I'll miss the mirth between us
When we close these pages and go

No Longer Apart

The two became one
They started as partners
Shortly after the fun had begun
They looked somewhat similar
They appeared both to agree
On the task they saw before them
What their joy would now be
So they took each other's hand
Placing them close to mutual heart
Headed now in true direction
Now one, no longer apart

Love on the Shelf

Our own little piece of Heaven
Our own tiny chunk of the crown
A time and space divided
A place to build our own little town

It's not quite the palace
That we left to buy our own
A bit short of everything
Among the feast, only a bone

We got what we asked for
A world of limit and sin
Built without love or peace
A tiny cubicle, a tiny bin

We get to be king of our kingdom
We have it all to ourselves
Trouble is, was it worth the making
Was it worth leaving love on the shelf

Included

By the hand of Christ, I pray
That I employ another day
By His gentle touch, I am warmed
Within His bosom, I will stay
Never let me see alone
A soul who belongs elsewhere
As part of the Christ in whole
Included
Concluded

By Christ

Can you just imagine the look
That you'd get from going this way
Putting words down on paper
And leaving them there to say
That what you see before you
Is eternal, starting today
It is written with the purest of intent
By a hand so finely hid
It is authored by my permit

In Poetic Terms

I see the world in poetic terms
I don't care to see it less
I'm accustomed to the texture
Of words that truly bless

I will see it my way
And you will see it yours
But I issue a minor clue
That mine is interior to yours

There is but one truth to know
Perception is stymied inter-dimensionally
With nowhere else to go

Take a look through my portal
Lend your sight to me
Behold the world in poetic terms
And open your eyes to see
A world redeemed of placement
In illusion seldom seen

Beyond Evolutionary

It's revolutionary, my friend
Way beyond evolutionary
It seeks its tepid home
To turn it into palace imperial
And to find a place of its own
Let's turn it on its head
This silly old world of ours
Come join the revolution
Be part of the patriot choir

Swanky Coat

A swanky coat doesn't matter
It's hardly worth a nod
All feathery and finery, I'm sure
But it doesn't amount to a lot

It may bedazzle and bedaze
It may twinkle in your eye
But it still won't amount to didley
Despite the curious eye

Learn to strip naked
Remove all barriers to love
Concentrate on the ethereal
Focus on Heaven above

It is a nudist colony there, I hear
Lots of bare butts and souls
Restating again in no uncertain terms
We don't need no stinkin swanky coat
To dress as one in turn

Dream Train

I say, I say
I really must say
What hops upon my dream train
And brings me this way
It's a cause extraordinaire
It's a miracle along the way
To see when that lonely dream train
Will bring me Home to stay

The Name on the Tomb

Live by the gun
Die by the gun
Ah hah, ah hah
Bound to have some fun

Let's shoot holes in each other
Let's open up some wounds
Take a look inside one
And determine the name on the tomb

Look inside your brother's wound
There to find your self entombed
Your name engraved in sterling words
Deep within your brother's terms

Christ Speaks

Christ speaks in many languages
Waiting to be heard
Displays in varied colors
The divine and Holy Word

He has spoken throughout the ages
Ever since time began
Often we have not heard Him
But now we truly can

For He speaks now and again
To those who have ears to listen
He appears to those of sight
He declares He is among us
Here to set us right

Pay heed now, dearest brother
For the Word has come to grace
The Mind that is forever
And shows us Christ as face

Looking

Hey, I know you
You look a lot like Christ
I'm looking at you
You looking at me
Asking ourselves
Who could this be
You know the answer, dear heart
It is the child of God
It is you and me
In Christ we see

Now and Forever

Now and forever
This is the term of my wait
To hold your precious hand
Embracing, with love, my fate

Same

All the same, all the same
All the same wonderful same
Alike and eternal at once
The same in the Infinite Same

We have all spent a lot of time
Playing in the worldly frame
Logged a lot of hours
Playing that silly game

A lot of different crap
That wasn't so different, I'm sure
A lot considered important
Yet nothing measured as pure

I'll opt for the latter
For pure I am certain to be
As pure as that Holy Sameness
That shows me truth to see

High Matters

I am involved in matters on high
It is becoming apparent to me
I'm not quite sure what to do about it
But, so far, it looks dreamy to see
My hope is to awaken
To the prize I know is fine
To fully see His Presence
To know His Will is mine

A Lovely Family

I just had a thousand babies
Gestation was quite profound
They just kept popping out
I loved them well, I found

What a lovely family
That has blossomed from this place
What a lovely family
I share with you its grace

Let's Do Lunch

Let's do lunch, shall we
It's been a year or two
It's time we got together
And shared a happy chew
It's been quite lonely
Without you, my friend
Let's do lunch real soon
It's time to make amends

No Regret to Follow Me Home

They are holy words, no doubt
I am simply amazed still
That I am the one
Who brought them about
I feel about as blessed
As a soul can possibly be
Honored that my Father
Does love and honor me so
If I died this instant
No regret would follow me Home

True Joining

You're wasting your time
With all this sex stuff, my friend
There is no way to connect
Bodies that never mend

There is however a joining
That will take your ecstasy far
The joining of mind and spirit
Is the nature of who we are

Sex is an effort in futility
Its pleasure a dubious drug
A distraction from love at best
A spurious little slug

I wish not to deny you pleasure
I simply refuse to see
Any such poor substitute
For the true joining of We

A Novel Fate

I'm about to write a novel
Of the poet's journey and such
Perhaps you'll deem to partake
And enjoy it very much
I certainly plan to
It looks like a lot of fun
To rummage about in that crazy attic
To relook at stories well spun
It ought to be a hoot
I can hardly make myself wait
We'll kick some past lives around
And see what determined my fate

Never Granted by Love

Sex is what we're taught to pursue
I know it feels real gooood
Money is mentioned in the game as well
I could spend it all profusely
To pay my way to hell
Fame might be your sweet appeal
I can only imagine how that must feel
Yet all I see come out of it
Is paltry and sorely unreal
For it will fleet and die
It will leave you holding the bag
Standing there with nothing to live for
Wondering where the thrills do lag
Why do they no longer
Grant you joy or love
I will tell you, my fellows
They were *never* granted by love

What You Need

Money nor sex nor fame
None shall be my game
I have played them all
And none have made me sane

I will simplify and be
All that I know I be
Simply being in love, I be
Now seeing all that is to see

Waste no more cycles
On cycles that pay no heed
To what enriches the soul
And gives you what you need

An All Purpose Pain

I've been sort of an all purpose pain
Never hurting to the extreme
Dabbled in trouble par excellence
But never with spirit so mean

I have hurt myself and others
I have gone against the grain
But I never wanted to harm anyone
Never wanted to issue pain

My harm has been both accidental
And incidental as well
The damage my life has done
Has never reflected well

My soul is redeemed by the fact
That none of it happened in truth
My mind stands clear and ready
To accept that golden truth

Just Do It

Don't name it
Just be it
Don't claim it
Just see it
Don't own it
Just love it
Don't fake it
Just do it

The Grandest Poem

The greatest poem ever written
Was never written at all
In fact, it was never spoken
Never upon ears to befall
It was more of a prayer really
Delivered in poetic form
More of a love of Father
That made it to the world of form

Some Stories to Tell

It is a course of sorts
This gentle word I write
Training for the heart
And all that brings us light

A path of roses strewn
Lightly across our path
Lilacs offering fragrant content
A vision of love at last

Take a poem with you, my friend
Reel it in and learn it well
When we meet again in Paradise
We'll have some stories to tell

A Kick in the Groin

Let's stop shooting each other
Cease and desist the hate
Let love replace it within us
Let us attend a better fate

Let us refrain from kicking
Each other square in the groin
Let us just drop the bullshit
Let the Brotherhood we join
Replace that which scorns us
And rents our soul for a coin

Let us know as brothers
All within our sight
Let us invite love in
And make our lives be right

Divine Gig

This gig is a divine assignment
The best thing I've ever done
All past efforts do fail
To equal the joy of this one

It's been quite the jolly adventure
That somehow I knew it would be
I have yet to be disappointed
In all that I have seen

I sense my Father's Presence
His nearness fills me with love
I'm thanking Him for the gig
As a gesture of His Love

No More Opinions

I no longer seek opinion
I have but truth to spell
Theory and conjecture no longer interest
My mind or what it can tell

I have found the center of the universe
Sweet love has found its home
Nothing in this world you could tell me
Could ever keep me from Home

So let the opinions fly
May they leave and never return
Leaving room now for salvation
Letting only truth be heard

Only Child

I'll see you on the other side
We'll meet with welcoming arms
Embrace and become each other
For once, we'll do no harm
For then, we'll be but Home
We will have found our way
Back to the Source that bred us
And keeps all harm at bay
He is our joy and protection
He is all that is worthwhile
He loves us beyond belief
We are His only Child

Straining Exquisite

It strains exquisite
This love around my heart
Threatening to burst the bubble
And explode myself apart
A unified presence will result
After that little self is gone
The larger, only Self
Remains as the Holy Son

Illusion Story

You had me at "The . . . ."
I was yours before you called
Ever have we been together
Before and after the fall

Inseparable we are, my brothers
All a part of the whole
United in truth beyond illusion
Despite the story we've been told

I'm sorry and not sorry
To say what I need to say
Yet all those years spent in illusion
We truly did lose our way

Yet you can't leave everything
Of that you are always part
So no matter that wasted in illusion
It could never tear us apart
Love is our only truth
Only it may fill our hearts

Paradise Sun

The only real pain is of separation
The declining of the Whole
All else is manifestation
Of mind's unwillingness to be home

Yet we truly have no choice
We are, divinely, who we are
We could no sooner leave ourselves
Than the heavens to deny their stars

It is only our belief that constrains us
The power of our own minds
We can decide to change them
Choose to be of our own kind

For we are the most holy
Of God's one and true Son
We have but ever departed
As rays of Paradise Sun

Beauregard the Beautiful

A black beauty he was
A long sought canine friend
Arrived shortly before the grim reaper
That took a son from them

Beau was his name
A black lab of short lived fame
Bringing joy and love
To the owners of the same

But the boy's death did take its toll
And left both parents in grief
Attend the young pup they could not
So they sought some friendly relief

A daughter did love him so
So into her care Beau went
The grieving parents sadly let go
Yet they knew it was love well spent

For sweet Heather would give him home
She would open up her heart
Beauregard would be well loved
Abiding within and never apart

Heather and Kim would give him care
They would love him long and well
Treasure him they surely would
Long after he left his shell

Heaven did take him
I know no other place
That such a sweet old friend
Could lay his loving face

Dedicated to our beloved and faithful friend
Sweet Beauregard, may your spirit never end

I'll miss you Beau, I wish I'd loved you mo

Evenings Poorly Spent

Now that I have you smiling
Wondering, what the hell's going on
This guy just yanked at my heartstrings
And next, he's putting me on

I will let you in on a secret
I will tell you the purpose of the tale
If you'll just pull on my finger
I'll explain all there is to tell

It might get crude for a second
I might even challenge *your* tale
But I'll never betray you to God
I would never cause you to fail

My heart is true, dear brother
My mind is of one intent
I no longer exhaust my evenings
In illusion poorly spent

Life Without Whimsy

What's a life without whimsy
A tit or tat for this or that
What's the sense of it
If we can't jiggle our fat
I take humor very seriously
I do little in casual jest
I don't really get the jokes
But I live my life with zest
For I have found sweet love
Embedded among the rest
Of all those silly jingles
Among my very best

Scribe and First Student

I am the scribe and first student
Of these lovely miracle rhymes
I feel most honored by this
It has become the best of times
We are equally touched by them
They grace us, one and all
Pay attention with me, my brothers
Let us obviate the fall
Ancient mysteries will be resolved
You will travel near and far
Your mind will open up to you
You will see your angel star
Sweet love will become you
It won't be long or far

Ego Farewell

You lyin sack of doo
I don't believe a word you say
You have led me down many errant paths
Always distorting my way
I decline to bid you well
Or even to say *adieu*
I'm just happy you're leaving
I'll forever never remember you

That Word

Do we really want to include *that* word
I'm jiggy with it either way
I'm just not so sure about *that* word
It may cause some mild dismay

I hope you trust us by now
To know we would never offend
Unless it was absolutely necessary
Unless you needed the hint

Either way, it's just a word
Images get in the way
Leave it as collection of letters
A riddle to mind your sway

Let it be just what it is
A belief of dubious repute
Our love belongs to better things
Than words we defend and refute

(*That* word originates in an ancient southern California dialect.
It is used exclusively to offend what we defend, and that's all)

Inseparable

We are one in the same
You may call us any name
We cannot separate the inseparable
We deserve a collective fame

See how powerless
We are in the world we reside
See how truly useless
Is all that we dearly prize

They are baubles at best, my friend
They may be hideous more
They hide that truly dear to us
They blind our priceless lore

When we drop these loveless rules
When we step up to the line
When we know we are inseparable
The part you will know as divine

From My Hand

Have you found your thousand miracles
I must say that I have done so
Bequeathed the instant I wrote them
Now to grace us forever more
They may not seem that way to you
Neither resonate nor appeal
But to me they are simple miracles
I ask for no repeal
I feel so blessed to be here
With this pen upon my hand
I ask you to take up the quill
I ask you to understand
That all that has eluded us
All that we need not demand
Are miracles in the making
That have emanated from my hand

Inane Conversation

Isn't there enough
Inane conversation
Haven't we far exceeded
A verbal consternation
Canned phrases and thoughts alike
A sound byte for the new age
Allowing the flow of banter
But nothing of spoken sage
If I see one more cliché
If I hear another phrase
I think I'll hurl it up
And enter a different phase
How about we talk about something
That can matter and save our lives
How about dropping all the bullshit
And watch our language come alive

Exploding Heads

If God gave me all right now
I'm thinking my head would explode
I've come quite near to it lately
I'm looking to finally decode
All that has been rightly given
All that I need to know

Too much of a good thing
Can blow your mind apart
Let our beloved Captain
Come and manage our start

I'll take all I can handle
I'll let the divine decide my way
I know the rest of my inheritance
Will be there when I can stay

Trinkets and a Rose

I seek no medals from earth
Nor do I need its commendation
I have found my center of value
I have discerned my divination

So many trinkets, so little value
Made to adorn and adopt
An attitude so self righteous
It's bound to be a flop

How could such lowly trinkets
Cause us to lose so much
Vehicles and structures alike
Distracting us from truth as such

I pray you find your value
Not in title or pose
I pray you see your holiness
I hope you'll accept this rose

The Path

Complete forgiveness
Leads to peace
Peace opens the door
To truth
Truth invites love in
Love unifies all
All is God

Temple Not

The body is temple not
It is mortuary indeed
An empty bucket apart
Only the self it feeds
An idol of loveless proportions
A symbol of ego's greed
A mirage and distraction of mind
Separation its only plea
Spend not your lonely hours
To make of it your creed
It offers next to nothing
It hides that which we need
A veil in the middle of thought
That blinds the Holy See

Our Father's Thoughts

The wonderful holy course
Born of blue and gold
It has taught me how to see
Conveying my sweet Savior's words
It has taught me how to be
I have waited so long for its knowledge
I have waited its voice to hear
Now that it has welcomed me
We hold each other dear
For it is more than ink and paper
More than we can see
It is a temple of truth
Our Father's Thoughts to read

Fleshy Outfit

I could forego a bath
And brush my teeth no more
Ignore my dental hygiene
Wear but dirty linens
Care not for rags or riches
Leave those pills upon the shelf
Care not for my appearance
Shun the public eye
And if all these things were done
They would diminish me not one bit
For I remain but Christ
No matter the fleshy outfit

I Run No More

I run no more
Now I fly
Bound no more
Soaring high

Getting larger
Expanding outward
Inward as well

Becoming much more
Than previous
Found at last
Home forevermore

What We Thought

So much more than thought
Greatness concealed in magnificence
Infinite the loss
Of wretched singularities
In trade for what we thought

Holy Thee

I want my head to explode
Take my leave and leave this place
I'd like to see me depart
And assume a holy face
Go where I'm going
Allow it simply to be
Become my true ancestor
My Father, Holy Thee

Take No Time

Do yourself a solid
Forego a tendered plea
Take a bite of this pie
Open up to me
Join me right away
Take no time to pause
Leave whatever you're doing
Bequeath no time for cause

Prior Poetry

Roses are red
Violets are blue
Ha, ha, ha
I love you

This was my prior poetry
This was what ego bought
Now I have raised my pen
Asking Christ to fill it again

Becoming somehow better
Divine, in fact, at times
More reason to the rhyme there is
A significantly better clime

So as you see, my friend
I was hapless and alone back then
Since I raised my pen
Christ writes with me again

The Best We Can Be

No nibbling or nit picking here
I'll tell you only relevance
To bring you ever near
And put aside your fears

If it's too much to swallow
Overload for brain and mind
Be at peace with whatever
Holiness you find

It will be sure and simple
The truth by any name
Taking away false identities
Fanning superfluous flames

So get in line, my brother
Hold the hand of your kindred soul
The best we can be is together
The best we can be is whole

Shakespeare in Rhyme

Shall we deem our brother William
Credit for all deserved
Or was it scribed by Sir Francis
Which was the writer's terms
The fruit, my friend
Is all that matters
The product of their faith
Roles are played in unison
By Christ, the bard so sayeth

Backdrop in Absurdity

It's a backdrop in absurdity
A wallpaper of dubious positioning
These lines of crude unacceptability
That haunts your ears and mind
Give them no quarter
They are simply words of rhyme
Just because they point out bullshit
Or fart or belch of any kind
Should not distract your sensibilities
From offense in lesser mind
So if you ever wondered
Just what the fuck I was doing
I was simply doing this, my friend
To amuse and question *your* musing

Brothers of the Same Mind

I am intentionally dissociating
From the world and body as such
I'm leaving the lesser mind behind
For the one with a golden touch
I could leave right now
And never look behind
For I know we will always be
Brothers of the same Mind

What You See

Be happy with what you see
It will tell you who you are
It is the inside of the envelope
It is that which you hide
It is the inner lining
Of the thoughts you bring to bear
Upon what you see as life
It is merely vivid illusion
The shadows of what we be
For Christ beyond the layers
Will see what is true to see

Merry Go Around

It's a silly old merry-go-round
This world we call our home
Lots of diverse reactions
Lots of ominous tones

It's not all that great, you know
As long as we see in dark
Lots of scary conditions
Little or no place to park

Yet lying above the scary
Away from the menacing tone
Exists a lovely merry-go-round
The one that is truly our Home

Love as Paint

With love as paint
I would brush but one bright hue
Containing each and every color
Containing both me and you
Blending as one, our colors
To form the magnificent hue
Forever painted together
In a portrait of glorious view

Beyond Words

What I have learned
Is beyond simple words
So I think I'll shut up now
And cease to be heard
I pray the same for you
I can't wait to see you go
Beyond these pale insufficient terms
To the place where you will know
Exactly what I'm talking about
And know that it is so

Voyeur

I've lived the life of a voyeur
Curious about the world
Wanting to see out
Without letting anyone see in

Safe within my blinded room
Behind the one way mirror of glass
Seeing all of you
Keeping me in shadows past

Fear has been my jailer
Refusing to let me out
Yet I am its employer
That's what it's all about

I have chosen imprisonment
No one has held the key
That opens the door to my heart
And frees the incarcerated me

Christ now offers me choice
He says with open heart
That I can be what I want to be
Prisoner and fugitive apart
Or I can be the Christ I am
And live in Creator's Heart

Pages of Gold

Five blank pages
All that appears to me
Five blank pages
All left for us to see

What will be the outcome
Of this fluid ink I flow
What will grace these pages
And tell us all we know

I bequeath them to the Holy Spirit
I ask that He do the same
Together we write our farewell
On blank pages and minds as well

I'm truly not going anywhere
That will be plain to see
But the little me is dying
And Christ is who I'll be

So thank you for the forum
And the words that graced them so
Thank you for the listening
And sharing these pages of gold

Completion

Father, Thy Will is my will
It is my only will
I await and treasure the moment
When it will be my fill
To lose myself in You
Is to find my Home at last
Be again Who I am
Coming to completion at last

Holy It

I believe in all of it
For I know the Source from whence it came
I understand most of it
In essence, it is the same

I love all of it
For I know the author's name
I will follow the will of it
To end in my Father's fame

It has been quite the grand message
Wrapped in poem and praise
The words have come in love
For Heaven, their goal to raise

They have warmed and provoked me
For you, I pray the same
I believe in all of it
It has made me wholly sane

Reassembled in Grace

Four poems on a Monday
Who would have ever thought
I would finish this beloved work
Just the way I ought

I truly must say, I've loved it
Every single letter I wrote
And to share it with you, my friends
Has been my warming coat

It has made me whole and well
It has opened mind and heart
It has shown me ways to Heaven
It has taken my soul apart
Reassembled it in grace
And bequeathed to my Father's Heart

Wax Poetic Again

One night two years ago
A man received a dream
Within that dream was a story
In poetic terms it framed

Nicobod and Icobod
Made themselves well shown
They started a bit of something
Had he only known

I guess he really did
Though the mind had granted *no*
I'm sure he truly knew
From whence the story was told

So the haggard man did write
A poem that would lead to more
He ended with over a thousand
And probably a couple of more

So here we close our adventure
A time together well spent
We'll hook up again in the summer
Wax poetic again, my friend

No Regrets

I will harbor no regrets when I leave here
My life has reached its crest
All those wasted years
Turned out to be what was best
They all played a part in shaping
The man I was to become
A man worthy of aligning
With the divine that would come
I spent some time in the finest of company
We had ourselves some fun
We joked, and laughed, and felt
The oneness that was true
He smiled and called me partner
He called me brother too
We came to be known as one
As Christ, the Son of God
It never stopped us however
It never even slowed us down
We kept on writing those odes
Til they ran me out of town
We'll never know for sure
Perhaps the time was right
To hand it over to God
To end the poet's light

Epilogue

This will be the last
You will hear, *musings* wise
This concludes our time in rhyme
I will forever keep open eyes
For if we meet again
In word or joyful rhyme
I will celebrate the occasion
And cherish in it endless time

www.ingramcontent.com/pod-product-compliance
Lightning Source LLC
Chambersburg PA
CBHW070500090426
42735CB00012B/2636